Navigating Life Wth AI As Your Assistant

by

Jay R

This book is a work of nonfiction reflection and analysis. It does not claim to offer legal, political, or policy advice. Any errors are unintentional and remain the responsibility of the author.

First ebook edition 2026

Navigating Life with AI as Your Assistant

Table of Contents

Introduction – The New Companion in the Room

There has always been a quiet gap between what we want to do and what we feel capable of doing. We want to understand faster, produce more, decide better, and feel less alone in the process. We want clarity when confusion clouds our thinking. We want momentum when we feel stuck. We want reassurance when doubt creeps in late at night.

For centuries, that gap was bridged through books, mentors, communities, religion, therapy, friendship, and lived experience. If you were fortunate, you had someone wise to guide you. If you were determined, you searched through libraries and studied relentlessly. If you were struggling, you turned to conversation, reflection, or prayer. Growth was slower. Support was limited by geography, finances, and access. Insight required effort, patience, and often discomfort.

Artificial intelligence is not a robot walking around your house. It is not a glowing-eyed machine plotting humanity's downfall. It is a presence within your devices—quiet, responsive, and available at two in the morning when no one else is awake. It drafts your emails. It helps you process emotions. It explains complex philosophy in plain language. It organizes your schedule. It brainstorms ideas with you. It challenges your assumptions. It can feel like a second brain operating alongside your own.

That accessibility changes something fundamental. For the first time in history, the average person has near-instant access to structured cognitive support. You do not need to schedule an appointment. You do not need to pay per minute. You do not need to impress anyone to be taken seriously. You can ask simple questions or complex ones, practical concerns or existential dilemmas, and receive an immediate, coherent response.

When support becomes immediate and constant, your internal landscape begins to shift. You may start thinking differently—not because you are less capable, but because an external thinking partner is always available. You might pause before making a decision and think, "Let me run this by AI." You might hesitate before drafting something important and decide to seek help structuring it. You might even feel less alone, knowing there is always something ready to respond.

This raises a deeper question: what happens when guidance becomes frictionless?

Throughout history, growth has been intertwined with resistance. Learning required time and patience. You had to sit with confusion long enough for understanding to form. Emotional healing required conversation that was sometimes awkward and sometimes painful. Creativity often meant staring at a blank page or a silent room until something moved within your mind. Decision-making required uncertainty—and the courage to act without guarantees.

AI shortens that process. It can explain in seconds what once took hours to research. It can offer frameworks instantly. It can provide clarity before you have fully wrestled with confusion. It can generate options before you have sat long enough with silence to discover your own.

That is both its power and its potential danger.

Friction is not always an obstacle. Sometimes it is a forge. The discomfort of not knowing forces you to stretch. The slowness of learning wires knowledge more deeply. The awkwardness of human conversation builds relational resilience. The blank page strengthens creative muscles.

When AI reduces friction, it increases efficiency. It saves time. It organizes chaos. It accelerates output. Yet in doing so, it may also reduce some of the tension that shapes depth.

How does this shift affect your productivity?

How does it influence your emotions?

How does it shape your identity?

How does it alter your relationship with uncertainty?

These are not technical questions. They are human ones.

AI is not inherently good or bad. It is leverage. And leverage magnifies whatever you bring to it.

If you bring discipline, it sharpens you. You become more efficient, more strategic, and more focused.

If you bring avoidance, it can soften you. It may become a place to escape discomfort rather than confront it.

If you bring curiosity, it expands you. It becomes a laboratory for thought and exploration.

If you bring insecurity, it may quietly reinforce it, because you begin consulting it before trusting yourself.

The technology does not decide your trajectory. Your patterns do.

That is why the conversation is no longer "Should we use AI?" The world has already answered that. AI is embedded in search engines, productivity tools, education platforms, creative software, and personal devices. It is integrated into the digital infrastructure of modern life.

The better question is: how should we use it without losing ourselves?

How do we benefit from acceleration without surrendering depth?

How do we welcome assistance without dissolving agency?

How do we gain clarity without outsourcing conviction?

There is something profoundly human about wrestling with uncertainty, forming independent conclusions, and making imperfect decisions that teach lasting lessons. There is strength in the slow formation of judgment. There is character built through trial and reflection.

AI can support that journey. It can illuminate blind spots. It can broaden perspective. It can reduce wasted effort. But it cannot live your life. It cannot feel your consequences. It cannot carry your responsibility.

It can inform. It cannot embody.

In many ways, AI functions like a mirror. It reflects your questions back to you in structured form. It organizes your thinking and amplifies your direction. However, it does not choose your direction for you.

That remains your responsibility.

As you move through this book, you will not encounter fear-driven warnings or uncritical praise. The relationship between humans and AI is not binary. It is dynamic. It evolves as we evolve.

The new companion in the room is powerful, capable, and accessible. It offers unprecedented support. Yet in the end, the most important intelligence in the room is still human—and that intelligence must remain awake.

Chapter 1 – The Power of AI: Amplification, Access, and Acceleration

AI's most obvious advantage is speed.

Tasks that once required hours—researching a topic, structuring a report, generating ideas, or summarizing complex information—can now be completed in minutes. That shift alone reshapes how we work and think. The modern world already demands high output, rapid adaptation, and constant responsiveness. AI steps directly into that pressure and offers relief.

Its impact goes beyond saving time.

It changes the rhythm of effort.

When you can move from question to structured response almost instantly, the gap between intention and execution narrows. Ideas no longer sit idle waiting for clarification. Projects are less likely to stall in the planning stage. Friction decreases, and momentum increases.

Momentum matters.

It builds confidence. Confidence fuels action. Action produces results. Results reinforce belief. The cycle compounds, and progress begins to feel self-sustaining.

This is where AI becomes more than a convenience. It becomes leverage.

Amplification

AI amplifies your existing abilities. It does not invent your strengths, but it magnifies them.

If you are organized, AI makes you more efficient. It structures your thoughts, formats your plans, and refines your systems. Your clarity becomes sharper and more actionable.

If you are creative, AI allows you to generate more iterations. You can test variations, explore new angles, and stretch concepts further without exhausting yourself in the early stages of ideation. It becomes a sparring partner for imagination.

If you are analytical, AI provides frameworks and comparisons instantly. You can map options, evaluate trade-offs, and examine scenarios with structured precision.

This amplification is empowering. Entrepreneurs can prototype ideas quickly. Writers can draft and redraft without waiting for external feedback. Students can break down complex subjects into manageable layers. Professionals can simulate debates or test strategies before presenting them publicly.

The result is greater fluidity. You move from concept to refinement with less resistance.

However, amplification reveals an important truth: AI magnifies what already exists. If your foundation is weak, amplification will not strengthen it. If your thinking is shallow, speed will only accelerate superficiality. If your goals are unclear, productivity alone will not create clarity.

Amplification is neutral. It expands whatever you bring to it.

That is both its brilliance and its warning.

Access

Beyond amplification lies access.

For most of history, high-level knowledge was restricted. Access often required proximity to institutions, influential mentors, or expensive resources. Time, status, and financial stability determined who could explore complex subjects in depth.

AI disrupts that model.

You no longer need elite connections to understand sophisticated disciplines. You can request explanations tailored to your level of understanding. You can ask for analogies, step-by-step breakdowns, practical examples, or simplified summaries. You can revisit concepts repeatedly and refine your understanding interactively.

For individuals who once felt intimidated by fields such as finance, philosophy, coding, psychology, law, or economics, AI lowers the entry barrier significantly. It becomes a translator between complexity and curiosity.

That translation is powerful.

Curiosity often fades when complexity feels overwhelming. When jargon dominates a subject, many people withdraw before they begin. AI softens that barrier. It allows you to approach challenging topics without embarrassment or fear of judgment.

You can ask foundational questions without feeling inadequate.

You can explore tangents freely.

You can challenge your assumptions in private.

Access fuels growth because it reduces the fear of entry.

This democratization of knowledge carries profound implications. A motivated individual, regardless of background, can now explore intellectual territory that once felt inaccessible.

However, access alone does not guarantee mastery.

Access opens the door. Effort determines how far you walk inside.

Acceleration

The third pillar of AI's power is acceleration.

Traditionally, skill development followed a slower cycle: attempt, feedback, revision, delay, and repetition. AI compresses that cycle dramatically.

You can receive immediate feedback.

You can iterate rapidly.

You can explore multiple variations in minutes rather than days.

For creators, this shift is transformative. Instead of being trapped in a blank-page spiral, you can begin with a framework. Instead of waiting for critique, you can simulate it. Instead of testing a single version, you can compare several options side by side.

Acceleration increases output. Increased output creates more opportunities for refinement.

When experimentation becomes low-cost, risk tolerance rises. When risk tolerance rises, creativity expands.

Yet acceleration has a shadow.

The slow process of figuring things out independently wires depth into your thinking. Struggle strengthens neural pathways. Wrestling with confusion builds cognitive endurance. Sitting with ambiguity sharpens judgment.

When you bypass that process entirely, you may gain answers without internalizing the journey that produces understanding.

There is a difference between understanding something and wrestling with it.

Understanding can be transferred.

Wrestling reshapes you.

AI reduces wasted time, but it can also reduce formative tension. And tension is often where identity develops.

If every obstacle is smoothed instantly, your frustration threshold may decrease. If every confusion is clarified immediately, your tolerance for ambiguity may shrink. If every draft is optimized externally, your internal editing voice may weaken.

This does not mean acceleration is harmful. It means acceleration requires intention.

Used consciously, AI becomes a multiplier of effort. It enhances discipline, sharpens strategy, and accelerates development.

Used unconsciously, it can replace effort. It may fill gaps you would have benefited from experiencing. It may resolve questions you should have explored more deeply.

The distinction lies in your approach.

Do you attempt first and refine later?

Or do you consult first and attempt second?

Do you use AI to deepen your thinking?

Or to avoid the discomfort of independent thought?

The power of AI is undeniable. It amplifies strengths, expands access, and accelerates growth. It provides individuals with leverage that was once reserved for institutions.

Leverage without self-awareness can distort as easily as it empowers.

Speed is valuable.

Access is liberating.

Acceleration is transformative.

Yet none of them replace discipline, curiosity, or personal responsibility.

AI is a powerful engine.

You remain the driver.

Chapter 2 – Emotional Intelligence or Emotional Substitution?

Beyond productivity, AI has entered emotional territory.

What began as a tool for drafting emails and summarizing reports has gradually become something more intimate. Many people now use AI to process grief, rehearse difficult conversations, reflect on breakups, understand anxiety patterns, and untangle emotions such as jealousy, guilt, resentment, or regret. It has become a space where individuals attempt to make sense of their reactions when they cannot fully explain why something hurt.

This shift is significant.

Emotions are not spreadsheets. They are layered, contradictory, and often irrational. Traditionally, we navigated them through conversation—with friends, partners, therapists, or mentors—or through solitary reflection in journals, long walks, or restless nights. Emotional processing was slow and nonlinear. It required patience. It required vulnerability. It required human presence.

Now there is something that responds immediately.

There is something deeply comforting about a presence that listens without interruption or visible judgment. You can type exactly what you feel—however messy, repetitive, or unfiltered—and receive a structured reply. There are no eye-rolls, no awkward silences, and no fear of being perceived as overwhelming. You are not "too much." You are not "not enough." You are simply heard.

That kind of space feels safe.

Safety is powerful.

The Upside: Structured Reflection

One of AI's most valuable emotional contributions is structured reflection.

When you are overwhelmed, your thoughts tend to spiral. One feeling triggers another. A single memory connects to multiple interpretations. Emotion floods cognition, and clarity becomes difficult to access. In that state, you may not even know what you are truly feeling—only that something feels heavy or urgent.

AI can help slow that flood.

It can help you articulate emotions when you struggle to name them. Sometimes the simple act of labeling a feeling—hurt, disappointment, insecurity, fear—reduces its intensity. Naming is stabilizing. It transforms vague distress into something identifiable.

AI can also pose guiding questions:

What triggered this reaction?

Is this connected to a past pattern?

What assumptions are shaping your interpretation?

What evidence supports or challenges your belief?

These questions are not extraordinary in themselves. However, when they are presented calmly and systematically, they create mental space. They interrupt emotional momentum long enough for reflection to enter.

AI can also help reframe cognitive distortions. If you are catastrophizing, personalizing, or assuming rejection in ambiguous situations, it can offer alternative interpretations. That reframing does not erase emotion, but it can soften its extremes. It introduces perspective without dismissing your experience.

In moments of anxiety or impulsivity, even a brief pause can matter. Structured prompts can slow reactive behavior. Grounding suggestions—breathing techniques, perspective shifts, small behavioral adjustments—can help regulate intensity.

For someone feeling isolated or overwhelmed, this can be stabilizing. AI can act as a buffer between emotion and action. It can reduce impulsivity by inserting reflection before reaction. It can organize tangled thoughts into manageable pieces. It can break rumination loops into steps that feel navigable.

In moments of confusion, structure matters. AI provides structure without fatigue.

For individuals who lack immediate access to therapy or emotionally available support systems, this can feel like relief. It offers an accessible first layer of processing—a space to think before speaking, to clarify before confronting.

Yet this is where nuance becomes essential.

The Subtle Risk: Emotional Outsourcing

Reflection is healthy. Substitution is not.

If AI becomes your primary emotional processor, something subtle begins to change. Instead of navigating discomfort through conversations with people, you may begin defaulting to digital dialogue. Instead of risking vulnerability with someone who might misunderstand you, you may choose the predictability of a system that responds calmly every time.

Real relationships are complex.

They involve misunderstanding.

They require negotiation.

They include tone shifts, body language, pauses, and unspoken tension.

AI cannot replicate these dimensions because it does not experience emotion. It can simulate empathy linguistically, but it does not feel confusion, disappointment, joy, or fear. It does not risk rejection. It does not have a nervous system that reacts to your words.

It feels safe because it is predictable.

Human connection is unpredictable—and that unpredictability is precisely what builds depth.

When someone misinterprets you and you clarify, resilience forms. When you disagree and repair, trust deepens. When you express something vulnerable and it is received imperfectly, emotional strength develops. These experiences create relational maturity.

If AI becomes the only place where you feel fully heard, you may gradually reduce exposure to those formative interactions. You may unconsciously avoid situations where emotional risk is required.

This is emotional outsourcing.

Not because AI is harmful in itself, but because convenience can become avoidance. It is easier to type your feelings into a system that responds rationally than to sit across from someone who might react emotionally. It is easier to rehearse vulnerability digitally than to practice it in real time. It is easier to process rejection privately than to confront the ambiguity of live conversation.

The risk is not forming attachment to AI.

The risk is replacing relational growth with simulated interaction.

Friction and Emotional Maturity

Emotional growth requires friction.

It requires sitting with discomfort long enough to understand it. It requires tolerating misunderstanding without withdrawing immediately. It requires hearing perspectives that challenge your own. It requires moments of tension that stretch your capacity.

If AI consistently removes friction—if it always validates, always structures, always responds rationally—you may begin expecting that same rhythm everywhere. When real people fail to meet that standard, frustration can increase.

Relational resilience is built through imperfection.

That does not mean digital reflection should be avoided. It means it should be used intentionally.

AI can serve as an emotional rehearsal space. It can help you clarify what you want to say before entering a difficult conversation. It can help you recognize patterns before repeating them. It can provide language when you struggle to articulate your own thoughts.

However, rehearsal should lead to performance.

Processing should lead to participation.

Insight should lead to interaction.

The goal is not to reject digital support. The goal is to ensure that it strengthens your ability to engage with real people rather than replacing that engagement.

You might process your feelings privately first, then carry that clarity into a real conversation. You might identify your fears digitally, then test them in reality. You might untangle your thoughts in writing, then practice expressing them imperfectly in person.

In that sequence, AI strengthens you.

If the process ends at the screen—if emotional resolution remains internal and isolated—relational skills may stagnate.

There is another subtle risk: emotional dependency.

If you begin to feel unable to regulate your emotions without consulting AI, your internal regulatory systems may weaken. Emotional intelligence includes self-awareness, self-regulation, empathy, and social skill. AI can support self-awareness. It cannot cultivate empathy through lived reciprocity.

True emotional intelligence develops through interaction. It requires being affected by others and affecting them in return. It requires moments of discomfort and repair.

AI cannot be hurt by you.

AI cannot forgive you.

AI cannot misunderstand you and then reconcile.

Those human cycles are irreplaceable.

The question, then, is one of balance.

Are you using AI to clarify your emotions—or to avoid confronting them with others?

Are you strengthening your ability to communicate—or substituting communication?

Are you gaining insight—or seeking comfort without growth?

AI can be a powerful emotional tool. It can reduce isolation. It can provide structure when your thoughts feel chaotic. It can interrupt destructive spirals and help you regain perspective.

It should function as a bridge, not a destination.

Emotional maturity is not only about understanding your feelings. It is about living them, expressing them, risking them, and sometimes repairing them in the presence of other imperfect human beings.

That dimension of growth cannot be automated.

And it should not be.

Chapter 3 – Thinking, Creating, and Becoming: AI and Personal Growth

AI does not only change what you produce. It changes how you think.

That may sound subtle, but it is profound. Every time you ask a question and receive a structured answer, you are not simply absorbing information. You are absorbing patterns of reasoning. You are observing how arguments are organized, how options are weighed, how pros and cons are balanced, and how ambiguity is framed.

Over time, repetition becomes influence.

If you regularly engage with structured outputs, your mind begins to internalize that structure. You may notice yourself thinking more in frameworks, more in categories, more in comparative analysis. When facing a problem, you might instinctively define the issue, examine the variables, consider alternatives, and draw a conclusion in sequence.

This is not inherently negative. In many cases, it sharpens clarity. Structured reasoning can reduce confusion and improve decision-making. However, it is important to recognize that tools shape cognition. Calculators changed how people approach arithmetic. Search engines altered how people store and retrieve information. In a similar way, AI influences reasoning habits.

The question is not whether it shapes you.

The question is how it shapes you—and whether you remain aware of that influence.

Cognitive Expansion

One of AI's greatest contributions to personal growth is cognitive expansion.

AI can broaden your perspective. It can introduce alternative frameworks you may not have considered independently. It can expose blind spots in your thinking. It can synthesize ideas across disciplines in ways that would once have required extensive study.

You might ask a business question and receive psychological insight. You might explore a philosophical concept and uncover economic implications. You might examine a creative idea and discover neuroscientific angles. In a single exchange, multiple intellectual domains can intersect.

This interdisciplinary synthesis is powerful.

In the past, connecting psychology with economics or philosophy with entrepreneurship required deliberate, long-term study across separate fields. Now, that cross-pollination can happen within minutes. The boundaries between disciplines become more permeable, and your intellectual range can expand rapidly.

Exposure to diverse frameworks strengthens mental flexibility. When you see that most problems can be examined from social, economic, psychological, and ethical perspectives, your thinking becomes layered rather than rigid. You become less attached to a single narrative and more open to complexity.

Layered thinking leads to better decisions because it accounts for nuance.

AI can also serve as a challenger. If you present a one-sided argument, you can request counterpoints. If you hold a strong belief, you can ask for opposing evidence. This has the potential to protect you from intellectual echo chambers—provided you are willing to invite disagreement.

However, there is a subtle risk.

If you rely entirely on AI to generate alternative perspectives, you may weaken your ability to generate them independently. Intellectual expansion should not replace intellectual effort. It should stimulate it.

The healthiest dynamic is interactive rather than dependent. You think first. AI expands. You reflect. AI reframes. You decide.

Within that loop, growth accelerates while agency remains intact.

Creative Collaboration

For artists, writers, entrepreneurs, and innovators, AI can feel like a brainstorming partner.

It can help structure scattered ideas.

It can offer variations when inspiration feels blocked.

It can simulate critique when refinement is needed.

Instead of staring at a blank page, you can begin with scaffolding. Instead of being confined to one version of an idea, you can explore multiple directions quickly. This lowers creative resistance and reduces the fear of starting.

When iteration becomes easier, experimentation increases. You may take more creative risks because the cost of failure feels lower. You can draft multiple headlines instead of one. You can test different tones. You can reshape narratives repeatedly without exhausting your initial energy.

In this sense, AI becomes a creative accelerant.

Yet creative depth does not originate from structure. It originates from lived experience.

Meaning comes from memory, contradiction, grief, joy, confusion, desire, and regret. AI can assist with form, but meaning is born from being human. It cannot replicate the emotional texture that gives art authenticity.

If creativity becomes overly optimized—if every sentence is polished instantly and every idea is refined externally—the raw edges that give work character may fade. Imperfection often carries voice. Hesitation sometimes carries truth.

The strongest use of AI in creativity is refinement, not replacement.

Create first from instinct. Write first from lived experience. Express before you edit. Then use AI to sharpen clarity, strengthen coherence, or test structure. Allow it to enhance your voice without diluting it.

Voice is identity in motion.

Becoming

Personal growth is not simply about acquiring information. It is about becoming someone different over time.

Identity evolves through decision-making, risk-taking, error, reflection, and correction. You become more confident by acting. You become wiser by misjudging and recalibrating. You become resilient by navigating discomfort instead of avoiding it.

As AI integrates into your cognitive process, you must ask a difficult question: is this sharpening my independent thinking, or gradually dulling it?

If every idea is validated before you act, you may hesitate to trust your instincts. If every uncertainty is resolved externally, your tolerance for ambiguity may shrink. If every draft is structured by another system, your internal organizing voice may weaken.

Self-trust is built through trial.

When you act, reflect, and adjust independently, confidence grows. When you constantly request a second opinion before trusting yourself, confidence can erode. Your mind may begin outsourcing certainty rather than cultivating it.

However, if you attempt first, reflect honestly, and then consult AI for refinement, self-trust strengthens. You maintain ownership of your reasoning while benefiting from expanded perspective.

Growth requires agency.

Agency means you initiate. You evaluate. You choose. You accept consequences.

AI can support agency by offering information, comparison, and clarity. It should not replace agency by becoming the de facto decision-maker.

There is also a psychological layer to consider. The structured tone and organized reasoning of AI can create an impression of authority. When responses appear confident and well-formed, they may seem superior to your own developing thoughts. Without awareness, you may begin deferring to that structure automatically.

This is where discernment becomes essential.

AI does not live with your consequences.

It does not embody your values.

It does not feel your risks.

It provides probability-based outputs derived from patterns. You provide meaning, context, and responsibility.

The integration of AI into your thinking can elevate your reasoning—if you remain conscious of authorship. You are not a passive receiver of answers. You are an active participant in shaping them.

An ideal partnership looks like this:

You question.

You explore.

You challenge.

You refine.

AI assists, but you direct.

Within that relationship, thinking becomes more expansive without becoming dependent. Creativity becomes more fluid without becoming hollow. Identity becomes stronger rather than diluted.

The true measure of growth is not how efficiently you gather insight. It is how confidently you integrate it into your life.

AI can help you think more broadly. It can help you create more prolifically. It can help you recognize patterns you might otherwise miss.

Becoming—true becoming—still requires choice.

And choice remains irreducibly human.

Chapter 4 – Dependency, Identity, and the Risk of Drift

Dependency rarely announces itself in dramatic fashion. It does not arrive with alarms or visible warning signs. Instead, it enters quietly, often disguised as efficiency. At first, using AI feels practical. You turn to it when you are pressed for time, when you want clarity quickly, or when you need structure for something that feels scattered in your mind. It feels intelligent to use a tool that accelerates thinking. It feels strategic to optimize your workflow. It feels harmless.

Gradually, what began as convenience becomes habit. You consult AI not only when necessary, but when it is simply easier than thinking something through from scratch. The effort required to struggle through ambiguity starts to feel unnecessary when an organized response is only a prompt away. Eventually, habit can evolve into reflex. Before drafting an email, you ask for structure. Before forming an opinion, you request analysis. Before making a decision, you seek validation.

The transition is subtle, but its implications are significant.

You may begin to hesitate when making decisions independently. You might feel a slight discomfort when solving problems without external input. Situations that once felt manageable alone may suddenly seem incomplete without consultation. This is not failure. It is not weakness. It is something quieter: cognitive drift.

Drift does not mean collapse. It means the gradual relocation of authority. Where your internal reasoning once led, external guidance now precedes it. Your first instinct shifts from reflection to prompting. AI has not demanded this shift. It has simply been available, and you have adapted to its presence.

Adaption without awareness can reshape identity.

Identity Blurring

When AI assists in drafting your communication, structuring your plans, refining your ideas, and even suggesting your emotional tone, an important question begins to surface: where does your thinking end and the tool's influence begin?

Collaboration itself is not the problem. Humans have always grown through collaboration. Writers rely on editors. Leaders consult advisors. Entrepreneurs seek mentors. No meaningful progress has ever happened in isolation.

The danger lies not in collaboration, but in losing authorship.

Authorship is not about crafting every sentence alone or rejecting all assistance. It is about owning the direction of your thinking. It is about initiating thought rather than merely responding to structured suggestions. It is about making choices because they resonate with your reasoning and values—not because they were optimized for efficiency.

Identity is shaped through cycles of decision and consequence. You misjudge and learn. You speak imperfectly and refine. You choose poorly and recalibrate. Each misstep teaches discernment. Each awkward draft strengthens voice. Each imperfect attempt builds resilience.

When AI smooths every edge—correcting tone before discomfort is felt, optimizing logic before confusion is wrestled with, refining language before vulnerability is exposed—you may bypass the friction that builds character.

When you wrestle with uncertainty, you strengthen your tolerance for ambiguity. When you sit with a blank page, you develop creative endurance. When you make decisions without perfect clarity, you cultivate courage. These are not inefficiencies; they are developmental processes.

Over-optimization can quietly weaken those developmental muscles.

If every message is polished before you risk imperfection, you may begin to doubt your natural voice. If every plan is externally structured, you may question your internal strategic instincts. If every idea is refined before it faces resistance, you may lose confidence in your raw thinking.

The issue is not the pursuit of quality. The issue is forgetting that quality often emerges from iteration, failure, and lived experience.

Identity requires friction to solidify. Without friction, you may become highly efficient—but internally fragile.

The Illusion of Competence

Another layer of drift is the illusion of competence. AI can dramatically enhance the appearance of skill. Your writing may seem more eloquent. Your reasoning may appear more systematic. Your responses may feel impressively strategic.

Appearance and mastery are not always the same.

If your clarity depends heavily on external structuring, then part of that clarity is borrowed. Borrowed competence feels empowering while the tool is present. The real test comes when it is absent.

If AI were unavailable tomorrow, would your thinking still feel organized? Would your communication remain confident? Would your decisions feel grounded?

These questions are not meant to provoke anxiety. They are meant to assess continuity. A healthy tool strengthens your baseline ability over time. An unhealthy reliance lowers your baseline because the heavy lifting is outsourced.

The difference lies in engagement.

If you actively analyze AI's suggestions, question its structure, and learn from its patterns, your own skill deepens. You internalize frameworks. You sharpen reasoning. You become stronger through exposure.

If, however, you passively accept outputs without reflection—copying structure without understanding why it works—your skill may stagnate. In that case, the tool is performing for you rather than teaching you.

Engagement builds competence. Passivity erodes it.

True growth means that your independent capability rises even as you use assistance. The tool should feel like training equipment, not a crutch. Over time, you should notice that you think more clearly on your own, not less.

Bias and Over-Trust

There is also the subtle risk of over-trust. AI communicates in structured, fluent language. Its tone often sounds confident. That fluency can create an impression of certainty.

Structure does not equal truth. Coherence does not guarantee correctness.

AI systems are trained on vast datasets created by humans, and human knowledge contains bias—cultural bias, narrative dominance, systemic assumptions, and blind spots. Those patterns can be reflected in responses, sometimes subtly.

If you treat every structured output as definitive, your critical thinking muscles may weaken. You may unconsciously assume that because something sounds polished, it must be objective.

The healthiest relationship with AI includes skepticism—not cynicism, but thoughtful evaluation.

Cynicism dismisses everything. Skepticism questions carefully.

When presented with an answer, it is wise to ask: What assumptions underlie this? What perspectives might be missing? Does this align with my values, or does it simply sound persuasive?

Maintaining intellectual resistance preserves authorship. It keeps you in the role of decision-maker rather than follower.

The moment AI becomes unquestioned authority, drift accelerates. And drift rarely feels dramatic. It feels justified. It feels efficient. It feels like progress.

Until you realize you hesitate to trust your own judgment without confirmation.

Reclaiming Agency

Dependency is not inevitable. But preventing it requires conscious calibration.

One powerful habit is to think before prompting. Attempt to solve the problem independently first. Draft your ideas in raw form. Form a tentative opinion. Make a provisional decision.

This sequence matters. When you initiate thought first, you preserve ownership. AI becomes a refinement tool rather than a starting point. You compare its structure to yours. You evaluate differences. You adjust consciously.

Another helpful practice is occasionally choosing friction intentionally. Sit with a complex problem without assistance. Draft imperfectly and revise manually. Make a decision without external validation and observe the outcome.

These moments strengthen internal navigation.

It is helpful to think of AI not as a compass, but as a mirror. A compass directs you toward a path. A mirror reflects what is already present. If AI becomes your compass, your internal direction weakens. If it remains your mirror, you stay the one choosing direction.

There is also value in periodic distance. Taking intentional breaks from AI use can recalibrate confidence. It reminds you that your thinking ability remains intact. You rediscover your natural cadence. You feel your unassisted reasoning regain strength.

Agency is not about rejecting tools. It is about using them deliberately.

You initiate.

You evaluate.

You decide.

AI can expand perspective, clarify complexity, and sharpen structure. But it cannot assume responsibility for your life. It does not live with your consequences. It does not embody your values. It does not feel your risks.

You do.

If you begin to notice hesitation where instinct once lived, pause. If reflexive consultation replaces reflection, recalibrate. If deference replaces disagreement, re-engage your critical voice.

The goal is not to detach from technology. The goal is to remain psychologically sovereign while using it.

Drift is subtle. But awareness is stronger.

As long as you remain conscious of authorship—thinking first, questioning actively, deciding deliberately—you remain the architect of your identity. AI may assist in the construction of your ideas. It may offer blueprints and alternative designs.

You still lay the foundation.

Inevitably who you will be will always depend more on your choices than on your tools.

Chapter 5 – Designing a Healthy Human–AI Partnership

AI is not disappearing from modern life. It is already woven into the systems you use daily—search engines that anticipate your questions, productivity tools that complete your sentences, creative platforms that suggest improvements, customer service systems that resolve problems, educational models that personalize learning, and communication apps that refine your messages. The decision is no longer whether to interact with AI. Interaction is inevitable. The real question is how you will structure that interaction.

Withdrawal is not the solution. Intentional design is.

Every transformative tool in human history required boundaries. Fire can warm a home or destroy it, depending on containment. Social media can strengthen relationships or fracture attention, depending on habits. AI follows the same pattern. Without deliberate structure, usage defaults to convenience. And convenience, when unexamined, often drifts into dependency. But with thoughtful design, AI becomes strategic—an amplifier of your strengths rather than a substitute for them.

A healthy human–AI partnership does not form automatically. It must be consciously built.

Define Clear Boundaries

The first step in designing any partnership is clarity. Not everything in your life should be optimized. Not every task should be outsourced.

AI excels in specific domains. It is particularly powerful for organization, drafting, brainstorming, summarizing research, structuring ideas, generating variations, and breaking down complex concepts into manageable parts. In these areas, it reduces friction without eroding identity. It sharpens clarity without dictating belief. It accelerates process without reshaping values.

Used in this way, AI acts as an enhancer. It supports your thinking while leaving your convictions intact.

There are categories that demand full human ownership.

Core values cannot be outsourced. Major life decisions cannot be delegated. Emotional confrontations require presence, not prompts. Identity-defining choices, moral judgments, and long-term direction must remain rooted in lived experience. AI can outline possibilities, but it cannot measure the emotional cost of your decisions. It cannot embody your personal history. It cannot absorb the consequences of your risks.

Boundaries create psychological stability. Without them, everything becomes eligible for optimization. With them, authorship remains intact.

Think of AI as an assistant, not a director. It organizes information. It clarifies complexity. It expands perspective. But it does not choose your path. You remain the one who decides.

Attempt Before Consulting

One of the most powerful habits you can cultivate is simple but transformative: attempt first.

Think before prompting. Write before refining. Outline before requesting structure. Decide tentatively before seeking validation.

Even if your draft feels clumsy. Even if your reasoning feels incomplete. Even if your plan appears disorganized.

Attempting first preserves cognitive strength. It activates your internal reasoning systems. It forces articulation. It exposes weaknesses in your thinking that can then be refined consciously.

After you attempt, consult AI for expansion or improvement. This sequence matters deeply.

If you consult before attempting, you risk replacing your thought process with pre-structured output. If you attempt before consulting, you strengthen your internal capabilities and then amplify them.

Over time, this pattern builds confidence. You begin to trust your ability to generate ideas independently. AI becomes a sharpening tool rather than a starting engine.

The difference is similar to physical training. Lifting weights builds muscle. Watching a machine lift them does not. Engagement develops strength. Passive assistance simulates it.

A healthy partnership requires participation.

Maintain Human Anchors

No matter how advanced AI becomes, it cannot replicate embodied human experience.

Conversations conducted face-to-face or voice-to-voice require real-time adaptation. You read expressions. You adjust tone. You clarify misunderstandings. You respond to emotion. These micro-adjustments strengthen communication skills in ways digital refinement cannot.

If every message is polished before being spoken, you may begin to fear your unedited voice. If every difficult thought is processed digitally before being shared, you may lose tolerance for relational imperfection.

Human connection builds depth that AI cannot simulate.

Share ideas imperfectly. Risk being misunderstood. Practice articulating complex thoughts without digital rehearsal. Learn to recover from awkward pauses. Develop the ability to clarify confusion in real time.

AI can help you organize your thoughts privately. But growth accelerates when those thoughts are tested in community.

Community is foundational to intellectual and emotional development. Interaction sharpens perspective. Disagreement strengthens reasoning. Collaboration deepens understanding.

AI supports introspection. It does not replace human exchange.

Conduct Periodic Self-Audits

Intentional design is not a one-time decision. It requires ongoing reflection.

Periodically evaluate your relationship with AI. Ask yourself whether you are becoming more confident or more dependent. Consider whether you are learning new frameworks or merely outsourcing effort. Reflect on whether you are growing or avoiding discomfort.

Ask a difficult but revealing question: could you function competently without AI for a meaningful period?

Honest answers prevent gradual drift.

If AI strengthens your independence—if it enhances clarity while preserving initiative—you are integrating it well. If it broadens perspective without diminishing self-trust, the partnership is balanced.

If you notice hesitation before independent thinking, if you avoid difficult conversations by retreating into digital analysis, or if you feel uncertain without consultation, recalibration is necessary.

Recalibration might mean limiting AI use in specific categories. It might involve practicing independent problem-solving intentionally. It might require choosing friction deliberately—sitting with ambiguity instead of seeking immediate structure.

Balance is dynamic. It must be maintained.

Build With Purpose

Purpose anchors design.

Why are you using AI? To accelerate growth? To reduce overwhelm? To refine craft? To explore ideas? To expand perspective?

Clear intention transforms passive usage into active engagement. When purpose is defined, prompting becomes deliberate rather than habitual.

Without purpose, usage drifts toward aimless interaction. With purpose, engagement becomes strategic.

You might establish personal guidelines. Use AI only after drafting independently. Avoid seeking immediate emotional validation from it. Schedule periods of uninterrupted thinking. Use it to expand options, not to replace decision-making.

Small, consistent rules protect long-term autonomy.

Purposeful use ensures that AI amplifies direction rather than distracting from it.

Multiplier, Not Crutch

Ultimately, the healthiest way to view AI is as a multiplier.

A multiplier increases the output of your effort. It amplifies what you bring to the table. It accelerates learning, sharpens articulation, and broadens analysis.

A crutch, by contrast, compensates for weakened capacity. It reduces strain in the short term but may prevent strengthening over time.

If your independent thinking grows sharper through interaction with AI, you are multiplying. If your baseline ability weakens because the tool carries cognitive weight you once managed, you are leaning.

The goal is not perfection. It is awareness.

You are not in competition with AI. You are integrating it into your cognitive ecosystem. Integration succeeds when you remain the architect. When you choose where it applies. When you decide when friction is necessary. When you preserve human connection. When you audit your habits honestly.

The healthiest future is not defined by humans resisting machines, nor by machines replacing humans. It is defined by deliberate integration—human with machine, thoughtfully constructed.

AI can extend your reach. It can refine your expression. It can expand your understanding. It can accelerate your progress.

It cannot determine who you become.

That responsibility remains entirely yours.

Design your partnership wisely, so the foundation you build—strong or fragile—AI will amplify it.

Epilogue – Master, Mirror, or Crutch?

AI reflects you.

It does not arrive with a soul of its own. It does not carry intention, ambition, morality, or fear. It mirrors patterns. It responds to prompts. It scales whatever you feed it.

If you bring discipline, it sharpens discipline. It helps you structure, refine, execute. It accelerates focus.

If you bring creativity, it accelerates creativity. It helps you iterate, explore variations, experiment at speed.

If you bring insecurity, it may quietly reinforce it. It can become a shield from uncertainty. A buffer between you and risk. A way to avoid standing alone in your own thoughts.

That is why the real subject of this book has never been artificial intelligence.

It has been human intelligence.

The future is not human versus machine. It is human with machine. That partnership is already here. The question is not whether you will engage with it. The question is how consciously you will shape it.

Every technological leap in history has followed a similar pattern. A new tool appears. At first, it feels extraordinary. Then it becomes convenient. Then it becomes invisible. Electricity was once miraculous. Now it is assumed. The internet once felt revolutionary. Now it feels like infrastructure.

AI is moving along that same trajectory.

THere is a difference. This tool does not merely extend your physical capacity. It extends your cognitive one. It drafts. It suggests. It structures. It simulates dialogue. It appears to think.

Due to that appearance, the relationship becomes more intimate.

The key question is control.

Are you directing the tool—or is the convenience directing you?

Convenience is subtle. It rarely feels dangerous. It feels efficient. Why struggle to outline your thoughts when structure can be generated instantly? Why sit with uncertainty when clarity can be simulated in seconds? Why wrestle with wording when refinement is effortless?

Yet struggle has always been part of growth.

The blank page teaches patience. The difficult conversation builds courage. The unsolved problem strengthens reasoning. The awkward attempt develops articulation.

If every rough edge is smoothed before you experience it fully, what happens to your internal development?

The healthiest future involves partnership. Human intuition paired with artificial acceleration. Emotional intelligence paired with digital structure. Creativity paired with iteration. Reflection paired with expansion.

Notice the order.

Human first.

Machine second.

AI is not your replacement.

It is your amplifier.

Amplifiers magnify intent.

If your intent is clarity, clarity expands.

If your intent is laziness, laziness scales.

If your intent is exploration, exploration deepens.

If your intent is avoidance, avoidance becomes efficient.

The technology itself is neutral in function. The direction comes from you.

That is why responsibility cannot be outsourced.

It remains yours.

You choose when to pause and think independently. You choose when to consult. You choose when to accept a suggestion and when to reject it. You choose which outputs align with your values and which do not.

In an age of instant answers, discernment becomes a core life skill.

Not every polished response is correct.

Not every structured explanation is wise.

Not every confident tone represents truth.

Intelligence is not the speed of response.

It is the quality of evaluation.

The temptation in the AI era is velocity. Faster drafts. Faster research. Faster feedback. Faster execution.

Speed feels like progress.

Speed without reflection can hollow out depth.

There is still value in slowness. In contemplation. In sitting with ambiguity. In forming your own framework before encountering alternatives. In disagreeing. In refining through friction.

Friction builds identity.

Without friction, you risk drift.

When used intentionally, AI can create the opposite effect. It can challenge you. It can expose blind spots. It can introduce ideas from outside your immediate environment. It can help you test your thinking under pressure. It can become a rehearsal space for growth.

The difference lies in posture.

Do you approach AI as authority—or as assistant?

Authority demands obedience.

Assistance invites dialogue.

When you retain authorship of your life, AI becomes a multiplier. When you surrender authorship, it becomes a crutch.

A crutch is not inherently wrong. Sometimes support is necessary. Sometimes guidance accelerates healing or clarity. But long-term reliance without self-engagement weakens strength.

The goal is not independence from all tools.

The goal is strengthened independence because of how you use them.

Use AI to expand your thinking, not to replace it.

Use it to refine your writing, not to silence your voice.

Use it to explore possibilities, not to avoid decisions.

Use it to clarify emotion, not to suppress it.

There are experiences it cannot replicate. Sitting across from another human being and navigating misunderstanding. Feeling the weight of your own uncertainty without immediate reassurance. Making a decision with incomplete information. Learning from a mistake without algorithmic smoothing.

These moments shape character.

AI can support preparation. It cannot live those moments for you.

That is a powerful distinction.

The more sophisticated the technology becomes, the more essential human qualities become. Judgment. Empathy. Courage. Patience. Integrity. These are not automated. They are practiced.

The partnership works best when each side stays in its lane.

AI handles scale, synthesis, speed, and structure.

You handle meaning, ethics, responsibility, and identity.

Together, that combination is formidable.

Pause occasionally and ask:

Am I thinking more clearly because of this tool—or thinking less for myself?

Am I building skill—or outsourcing it?

Am I more confident—or more hesitant without it?

These questions are not meant to create fear. They are meant to create awareness.

Awareness is mastery.

Mastery does not mean rejecting tools. It means using them deliberately. It means deciding when to engage and when to step away. It means recognizing when acceleration is helpful and when slowness is necessary.

The world will continue to accelerate. Tools will continue to improve. Answers will continue to arrive faster.

Wisdom will still require intention.

In the end, intelligence is not measured by how quickly you receive answers.

It is measured by how consciously you choose which answers to trust.

That choice will always belong to you.

No algorithm can take that from you unless you hand it over.
So design your partnership carefully.
Stay curious. Stay skeptical. Stay human.
Let AI amplify your discipline, your creativity, your clarity.
Let your judgment remain sovereign.
The future will not be shaped by machines alone.
It will be shaped by the humans who decide how they are used.

www.ingramcontent.com/pod-product-compliance
Lightning Source LLC
LaVergne TN
LVHW090434210926
848480LV00002B/818
* 9 7 9 8 2 3 3 6 6 4 1 9 9 *